Q&A Kids

WEATHER

AMY CHAPMAN

ANGELIKA SCUDAMORE

WINDMILL BOOKS

Published in 2026 by Windmill Books, an Imprint of Rosen Publishing
2544 Clinton St.
Buffalo, NY 14224

First published in Great Britain in 2026 by Wayland

Editor: Sarah Peutrill
Designer: Lisa Peacock

Some of the text in this book was first published in Fact Cat: Weather by Izzi Howell

Cataloging-in-Publication Data

Names: Chapman, Amy, author. | Scudamore, Angelika, illustrator.
Title: Weather / Amy Chapman, illustrated by Angelika Scudamore.
Description: Buffalo, NY : Windmill Books, 2026. | Series: Q & A kids | Includes glossary and index.
Identifiers: ISBN 9781725396401 (pbk.) | ISBN 9781725396418 (library bound) | ISBN 9781725396425 (ebook)
Subjects: LCSH: Weather--Juvenile literature. | Climatic changes--Juvenile literature. | Climatology--Juvenile literature.
Classification: LCC QC981.3 C437 2026 | DDC 551.6--dc23

Printed in the United States of America

CPSIA Compliance Information: Batch #CSWM26
For Further Information contact Rosen Publishing at 1-800-237-9932

CONTENTS

Can you spot the friendly gray clouds in this book? There are 13 to find, not counting me.

WEATHER

Q. What is weather?

A. Weather is the name that we give to temperature and outdoor conditions, such as rain and wind. The weather is always changing and is usually different every day.

Weather changes throughout the year depending on what season it is. There are four seasons in a year – spring, summer, autumn, and winter. Each season has different types of weather, but they often overlap.

LOOK AT IT

What is the weather like in each of these places? What do you notice about the clothes people are wearing?

A.

B.

C.

D.

SUNSHINE

Q. Is it always hot when the Sun shines?

A. The Sun shines every day, even in winter when days feel cooler.

Sunshine comes from the Sun. The Sun is the closest star to Earth. The Sun is so hot that its light and heat can be seen and felt on Earth.

The Sun shines every day in most places on Earth. In places close to the equator, the sunshine is stronger and hotter because these areas are nearer to the Sun.

FIND IT

These people are out on a warm summer's day. Spot four things that people like to do in warm weather.

CLOUDS

Q. What are clouds made from?

A. Clouds are made of water vapor. The water in seas and rivers turns into water vapor when it is heated by the Sun. This water vapor rises into the sky, where it forms clouds.

There are many types of cloud. Cumulus (say *kyoom-yew-luss*) clouds are puffy. Cirrus (say *sih-rus*) clouds look like long strings in the sky.

Some clouds form close to the ground. Other clouds (such as cirrus clouds) form high in the sky. Cirrus clouds are found at heights of 16,400 feet (5,000 m) above the ground.

Clouds that are close to the ground are called mist or fog.

FIND IT

Can you work out which are the cumulus and cirrus clouds in the picture?

RAIN

Q. When does rain fall?

A. When water vapor in clouds cools down, it turns into drops of water. Sometimes these drops of water fall from clouds as rain.

In some parts of the world, it rains from time to time in every season. In other places, it rains heavily during the rainy season.

It rains almost every day in tropical rainforests.

THINK ABOUT IT

Why does it take a long time for rain to reach the ground in rainforests?

WIND

Q. Can you see wind?

A. No, we can't see wind, although it is always there! Wind is moving air. We can feel wind though as it blows against our skin. We can also see things moving as the wind blows against them.

It can be important to know the speed and direction of wind. Strong winds can blow an airplane off course or even damage buildings.

Wind can be useful too. We can make electricity from wind. When the wind makes the blades on these wind turbines move around, they produce electricity. We use electricity to power lights and machines.

THINK ABOUT IT

Strong wind is sometimes called a gale. What kind of wind is a breeze?

STORMS

Q. Are all storms really noisy?

A. Some strorms are louder than others. In a storm, it rains heavily and there are strong, fast-moving winds. These winds can be dangerous, as they can knock over trees and blow things around. Storm clouds are dark gray and full of rain.

In thunderstorms, you can see flashes of lightning and hear thunder. Lightning happens when there is electricity in clouds.

FIND OUT
We always see lightning before we hear thunder. Why is this?

SNOW

Q. What is snow?

A. Snowflakes are made of ice crystals (lots of frozen drops of water joined together). Snowflakes are very small but there are around two hundred ice crystals in every snowflake! They can only be seen clearly through a microscope.

When the temperature in the sky is cold, water freezes inside clouds. If it is also cold on the ground, frozen water falls from the clouds as snow.

In some places, a thick layer of snow covers the ground in winter.

FIND IT

Can you find four things that we often link to winter?

ICE

Q. What makes ice form?

A. When the temperature drops below 32 degrees Fahrenheit (0 °C), water freezes into ice. Ice is hard, smooth, and very cold. Usually only the water on the surface of lakes and rivers freezes into ice. The water beneath is still liquid.

When lakes and rivers freeze in cold weather, birds such as ducks stand on the ice.

THINK ABOUT IT

The fresh water in the lake is frozen, but water in the sea is not. Why do you think that is?

DANGEROUS WEATHER

Q. What are tornadoes?

A. Tornadoes happen when strong winds spin inside a storm cloud. These spinning winds make a column that moves across the ground.

Tornadoes can spin at up to 310 miles per hour (500 km/hr). Tornadoes are very dangerous. They often destroy trees and houses. Some countries, such as the United States and Canada, have many more tornadoes than other countries in the world.

MATCH IT

There are four different dangerous weather events here. But the labels are mixed up. Can you sort them out?

A.
Fog

B.
Floods

C.
Tornado

D.
Hail

WEATHER FORECASTING

Q. How do weather forecasters know what the weather is going to be?

A. Satellites above Earth collect information about the weather from space. This information is sent to computers to help weather forecasters work out the weather ahead.

Weather forecasting is a difficult job because the weather is always changing. Weather forecasters prepare charts with symbols for television, radio, newspapers, and the Internet. They show us what weather might happen in the next few days.

SORT IT

Look at the weather symbols. Can you help Emma and Joe work out what kind of weather each one shows?

A.
B.
C.
D.
E.
F.

WEATHER AND LIFESTYLES

Q. How does weather affect the way people live?

A. The weather affects lots of things, such as how much time people spend outdoors and what plants they grow.

The weather in some places is hot and dry in summer and warm and wet in winter. This weather is just right for farmers to grow fruits, such as grapes, oranges, and lemons.

Other places have short, cool summers and long, cold winters. In some of these places, shopping centers are underground.This helps people to avoid the harsh winter weather.

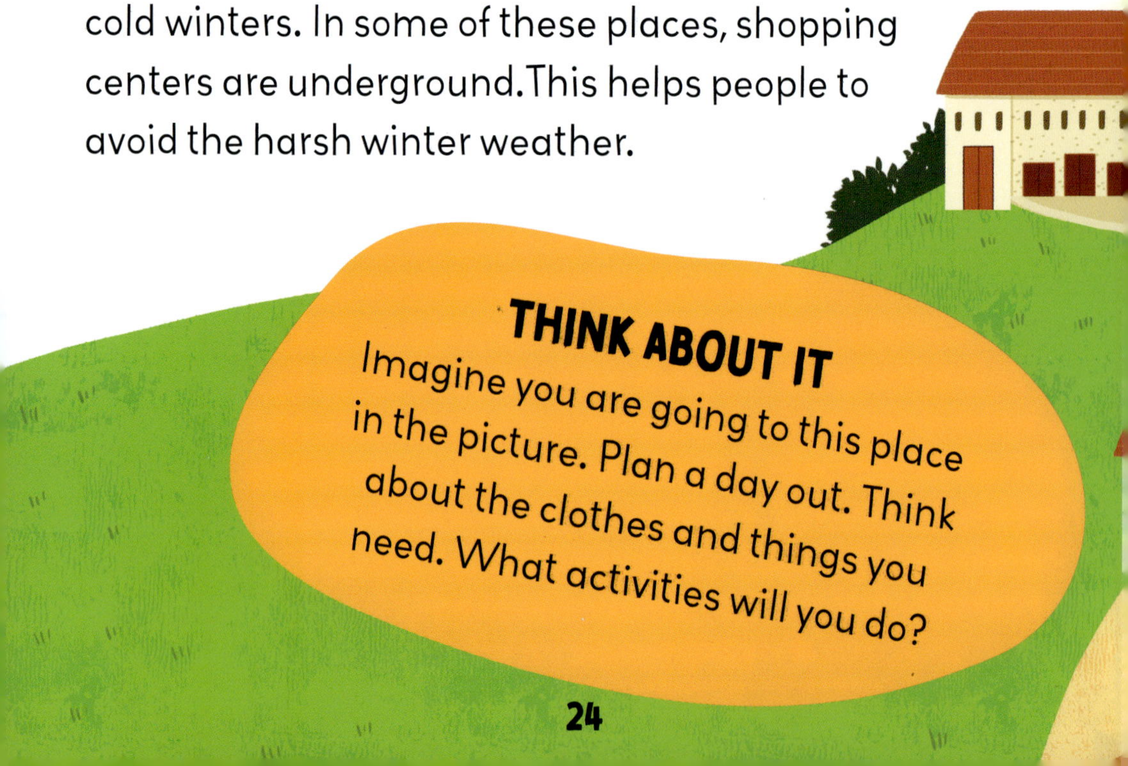

THINK ABOUT IT

Imagine you are going to this place in the picture. Plan a day out. Think about the clothes and things you need. What activities will you do?

ADAPTING TO WEATHER

Q. What other things are affected by weather?

A. So much! The design of the houses people live in, the clothes they wear, what they eat, and the jobs they do are affected by local weather.

Where there is warm sunshine, tourists come to sunbathe and swim. Some people work in the mornings and evenings and rest in the daytime.

Where it is cold all year round, houses have sloping roofs for snow to slide off. People wear thick clothes.

THINK ABOUT IT

How has this place been designed by people for the weather?

CHANGING CLIMATES

Q. Why are people talking about the climate on Earth changing?

A. The climate on Earth has been changing very slowly over millions of years. Now it is changing more quickly because of things people are doing such as burning fossil fuels.

We call this change global warming and it is causing more extreme weather. In some places, there are more heatwaves and droughts.
In others, there are more storms and floods.

As well as affecting people, changing weather also affects plants and animals.

FIND OUT

Choose some of the plants and animals in this picture. Find out how changing climates affect them.

Monarch butterfly

Apple

Oak tree

Wheat

Giant panda

Bee

Polar bear

Elephant

Puffin

Leatherback turtle

Jaguar

QUIZ

1. The Sun is a planet. True or not true?

a) true

b) not true

2. Clouds are made of water vapor. True or not true?

a) true

b) not true

3. In which habitat does it rain nearly everyday?

a) desert

b) rainforest

c) seashore

4. We hear thunder before we see lightning. True or not true?

a) true

b) not true

5. At which temperature does water freeze?

a) 50 degrees Fahrenheit

b) 35 degrees Fahrenheit

c) 32 degrees Fahrenheit

6. What is a tornado?

a) a spinning column of wind

b) a large piece of ice

c) a storm with thunder and lightning

Quiz answers

1. not true – it is a star.
2. a – true
3. b – rainforest
4. b – not true – we see lightning before we hear thunder
5. c – 32 degrees Fahrenheit
6. a – a spinning column of wind

GLOSSARY

column something with a tall, narrow shape

conditions the temperature and weather in an area

crystal a transparent substance that has become solid

destroy to damage something so badly that it doesn't exist anymore

drought a long period of time without any rain

electricity energy that produces light and heat and can be used to power machines

equator an imaginary line around the middle of the Earth

fossil fuels fuels such as oil or coal that formed from animals and plants that lived millions of years ago

freeze to turn hard and solid because of the cold

heatwave a period of time with unusually hot weather

ice frozen water

microscope a machine that makes small objects look bigger

on record describes something that has been officially measured and written down

power to give electricity to a machine to make it work

spin to turn around quickly

surface the top part of something

temperature how hot or cold something is

tropical rainforest one of the rainforests that grow close to the equator

water vapor many small drops of water in the air

INDEX

SOME ANSWERS

p. 4 A. hot weather/cool clothes; B. windy, cooler weather/warmer clothes; C. warm but not hot weather/ trousers, not shorts but no need for a coat; D. cold weather/very warm clothes.
p. 6 Go on picnics, eat ice pops, cool off in a sprinkler, sunbathe
p. 8 Cumulus clouds at the top; cirrus clouds below
p. 10 The leaves slow down the rain's journey to the ground.
p. 12 A breeze is a gentle wind.
p.15 Light travels faster than sound.
p. 16 Snow, cold weather, warm clothes, and hot drinks
p. 19 Salt water freezes at a lower temperature than fresh water.
p. 20 A. floods; B. tornado; C. hail; D. fog
p. 22 A. cloudy weather; B. rain; C. snow; D. sunshine; E. thunderstorm; F. strong winds
p. 26 People have built houses with sloping roofs to allow snow to slide off, they have built a ski resort for the snow, and built cable cars to carry skiers and walkers up the mountain.